OUR QUEST TO KNOW THE MEANING OF LIFE

A Philosophical Reflection

By

H. A. Shirantha Madushan Perera

"To my parents, teachers and friends who have always been my biggest supporters, my unwavering source of inspiration, and the reason I kept going even when the going got tough. Your love, kindness, and unwavering belief in me have meant the world, and I could not have done this without you. This book is dedicated to you, with all my heart and gratitude.".

Contents

CONTENTS

Foreword

In a world full of noise and distractions, it's easy to lose sight of what truly matters in life. We are constantly bombarded with messages that tell us what to do, what to think, and how to live. Yet, in the midst of this chaos, one question persists: what is the meaning of my life?

This is a question that has puzzled philosophers, scientists, writers, and everyday people for centuries. It's a question that speaks to the very essence of who we are, and what we hope to accomplish during our time on this earth. It's a question that demands an answer, yet one that is never fully answered.

In this book, the author takes us on a journey of self-discovery, exploring the different facets of this fundamental question. Through a combination of personal reflection and philosophical inquiry, the author invites us to delve deeper into the meaning of our lives, to uncover our purpose, values, and beliefs, and to discover what truly makes us happy.

Drawing upon the wisdom of great thinkers and the experiences of inspiring individuals, the author provides a roadmap for all of us who are searching for meaning and purpose. Through their stories, we learn that the quest for meaning is not an easy one, but it is a necessary one. We discover that we are not alone in our search, and that there are many others who have come before us, and who will come after us, in this journey of self-discovery.

This book is a call to action, an invitation to embark on a journey of self-discovery and to find meaning and purpose in our lives. It is a reminder that life is short, and that we have a responsibility to make the most of the time we have been given. It is a celebration of the human spirit, and a tribute to all those who have gone before us, in their quest for meaning and purpose.

I hope you enjoy reading this book, and that it inspires you to continue your own journey of self-discovery. May it guide you towards a life of meaning, purpose, and fulfillment.

H. A. Shirantha Madushan Perera

Assam Don Bosco University, Tapesia

2023. 03. 16

Preface

The quest for the meaning of life is an age-old pursuit, one that has puzzled and inspired human beings throughout history. As we navigate our way through life, we are often faced with difficult questions about the purpose and meaning of our existence. This book aims to explore the problem of "Man's Quest to Know the Meaning of Life" through a philosophical lens.

In this research, we delve into the human nature of the 'human person' and the innate desire to know and understand the world around us. We examine the complex interplay between our rational nature, our emotions, and our experiences, all of which shape our individual perspectives on life. We also explore the challenges we face when grappling with uncertainties, miseries, hatred, sufferings, and loss of hope, and how these experiences can impact our understanding of life's meaning.

Through this work, we hope to provide insight into the multifaceted nature of the human experience and offer a fresh perspective on the age-old question of the meaning of life. It is our belief that by exploring this topic in depth, we can deepen our understanding of ourselves, our world, and the importance of embracing the present moment. We invite you to join us on this journey of self-discovery and philosophical inquiry.

Acknowledgments

Writing a book is not a solitary activity, and I am grateful for the support and encouragement of many people who helped bring this project to fruition. First and foremost, I would like to express my deep appreciation to my dear parents, who have been a constant source of encouragement and inspiration throughout this journey. Their unwavering belief in me and this project has kept me motivated even when the going got tough. I would also like to thank my friends for their valuable feedback, expert guidance, and constructive criticism, which has helped me refine and improve the manuscript. Their contributions have been invaluable and have made this book possible. I would also like to thank Martha R Sangma for her assistance in various aspects of the book production process, including research, editing, and design. Her expertise and attention to detail have been invaluable.

Finally, I would like to express my gratitude to the many people who have inspired me throughout my life, both personally and professionally. Their wisdom, insights, and experiences have helped shape my worldview and have informed the ideas presented in this book.

Thank you all for your support and for being a part of this journey.

Introduction

I often wonder 'what is the meaning of my life?' and I know that I am not alone when I raise this question. Throughout the ages, philosophers have considered it to be the most fundamental question. Scientists, historians, philosophers, writers, psychologists and the common man, all wrestle with this question at some point in their lives. In fact, this fundamental question refers to a set of interrelated questions concerning purpose, values, and the good life: Who am I? Where am I going? What should I do with my life? What are the sources of meaning? Do I create meaning from within myself? What kind of values and beliefs should direct my life? What is my worldview? What is my philosophy of life? And so forth. This is a 'quest,' a hunger, a desire and a never-ending longing, that resides deep down in my being. This quest stares at me, taunts me, demanding an answer.

On the one hand, when this quest is not attempted to quench, man is unable comprehend his world and his place in the world, and the results are apt to be traumatic and unimaginable. Unfortunately, the traumatic and the unimaginable results have become daily occurrences today. Consider for instance, the people, who engage in violence and other forms of destructive behaviour against the human dignity. These men had lost the sense of meaning in their life and stumble through life to the very edge of the abyss. On the other hand, we find people who continued their 'quest' to know the meaning of life until their last breath. They all have interesting life stories containing a lesson to teach for the present and the next generations to come. Their 'quest,' in search of the meaning of life invites us to continue the journey they began. Consider for instance, the inspiring personalities such as Francis of Assisi, Don Bosco, Mother Teresa, Mahatma Gandhi, Nelson Mandela, and Pope John Paul II, who attempted to go against the current and make their lives meaningful, both in thought and in action.

Although the response to the quest differs from person to person, the fundamental 'quest' is present in our human nature. Therefore, we cannot neglect this quest. We have to attend to this quest understanding our position in the universe. First, my attempt in this paper is to present why man's 'quest' to know the meaning of his life unlike other living beings. Second, I want to suggest possible ways to quench this thirst. I accept the fact, that there are abundant researches made on this fundamental question in different fields of studies. But I feel compelled to do a research of my own to address it from a holistic philosophical approach with a historical overview. Throughout the research, I use the word "man" in generic sense, meaning "human being," not man in the sense of distinguished from woman.

In the first chapter, under the first subheading, I introduce the reasons for man's quest, taking human nature into consideration. First, I distinguish man, from other living beings, with his unique nature. Second, I consider, his rational capacity, which is endowed with intelligence, freewill, and consciousness. Third, I develop the concept of 'man' into the concept of 'human person.' Moreover, under the second subheading I intend to analyse man's moral behaviour. This is done in order to examine why man acts according to his passions, despite his orientation towards virtuous life.

In the second chapter, I focus on man's never ending quest for knowledge and truth. We all, as human persons, have both the 'quest' and the duty to know the truth and the meaning of our lives. Hence, throughout the history, we have attempted to arrive at the truth by unravelling the mysteries of the universe through scientific experimentations and philosophical argumentations. Yet we have not found a final answer. In this research, to discuss all scientific experimentations and philosophical argumentations will result in endless pages of inquiry. Therefore, in this chapter, I limit my discussion, only to epistemological dispute to arrive at truth. In the third chapter, I discuss the possible ways to quench our unending quest. First, I present the modern views, put forward by existentialistic and personalistic thinkers on human life. Second, I present the anthropological answer and different religious perspectives as avenues to find meaning to life. Here, my decision to discuss the religious perspectives, at last, has a reason. It is, because, there are unfathomable realities and mysteries in our universe, that need explanation. And our 'quest to know the meaning of life' is one of them. Religions in general provide explanation and answers to these unfathomable realities. For this analysis I consider only the four major religions, namely, Hinduism, Buddhism, Islam, and Christianity, expecting the best possible answer.

Chapter One

THE NATURE OF HUMAN PERSON

The first chapter of this inquiry is devoted to introducing the nature of human person in order to present the reasons for his persistent 'quest.' Thus, it is developed under the following subheadings. The first subheading places man at the highest mode of being among other living beings because of his unique human nature. The second subheading considers man's moral behaviour to see if he lives up to his proper human nature.

1. Human person's higher nature in the world

Man has been the subject of various philosophical schools of thought and can be seen as the centre of every philosophical inquiry. Moreover, the nature of the human person is also vital and crucial in his being in the world. Therefore, it has been the subject matter of many sciences including, biochemistry, psychology, sociology and anthropology. However, a proper definition to define the unique nature of the human person is yet to be found. In accordance with the recent anthropological researches, man's nature constitutes of certain aspects, which disclose to us that he is material, rational and spiritual in his being.[1] In this chapter, my concern is not to give a definition to his nature, but to use some of the vital characteristics of his nature to understand why man quests for meaning of his life, when other living beings just exists. Thus, let me make an attempt to distinguish man's unique nature in general, comparing him with other living beings in the world.

1.1. Man among other creatures

Man is a living and thinking organism. He is traditionally known to be the cream of creation for his unique nature, which set him apart from other living beings in the world. Therefore, man's unique nature among other creatures is straightforward to distinguish for many reasons. First of all, by the unique evolution of the brain man wins a higher place in the hierarchical order of beings.[2] Man does certain things which no other animal could do.

For instance, modern scientists together with Charles Darwin would agree, that only Homo

---

[1] James Urry, "History of Anthropology" in, *The Routledge Encyclopaedia of Social and Cultural Anthropology,* 2nd ed. Alan Barnard and Jonathan Spencer, New York, Routledge Publishers, 2010, 349.
[2] Folliet Joseph, *Man in Society*, London, William Clowes Limited, 1963, 7.

sapiens in the evolution theory had the capacity and capability to change a stone into a tool, or to wonder about the stars in the starry heavens and ultimately become self-conscious of his existence.[3] This makes us clear, that man alone has this unique gift of reasoning ability and abstract intelligence to be aware of his consciousness.[4]

Another way of distinguishing human person's unique nature from other animal is by the social behaviour, which makes him possible the communication and transmission of knowledge from generation to generation. This knowledge is vastly superior to that of other species.[5] While animals do communicate with one another, their communication is very limited. They are unable to communicate ideas and information pertaining to past or future, for they are aware only at the present situation. But man, alone has the power to think at any time due to his capacity for abstraction. In line with this, John Locke in his celebrated thesis, An Essay Concerning Human Understanding remarks that "it is the understanding that sets man above the rest of sensible beings, and give him all advantages

---

[3]George Paul, *"Philosophical Anthropology"* in, Encyclopedia Britannica, Vol. 25,15th ed. Chicago, Encyclopaedia Britannica publishers, 1997, 554.
[4] Christen C. Young and Mark A. Largent, *Evolution and Creationism,* London: Green Wood Press, 2007, 202.
[5] Joseph, Man in Society, 7.

and dominion which he has over them..."[6] Though man differs from his so called higher faculties he is one with animals and plants in his vegetative state. The vegetative functions are indispensable to humans as to all other living beings.[7]

1.2. The capacity to reason

The explanatory notion of rationality in man refers to certain intellectual capacities like imagination, memory, and the ability to use language. All these are made possible because of man's rational capacity. Moreover, man talks, thinks, and deliberates. Ever since man came to the world, he kept on improving and developing because of his rational capacities unlike other living beings which do not possess the gift of rationality. For instance, man transformed his cave into skyscrapers while the birds make the same nest all through their generations.[8]

The rational dimension of human person is divided into two faculties namely, intellect and will.

---

[6] John Locke. *An Essay Concerning Human Understanding*, ed. and intro. by John w. Yolton, London, J.M. Dent Ltd, 1992, 1.

[7] Pico Della Mirandola, *On the Dignity of Man,* tr. in English, Charles Glenn and Douglas Carmichael, Cambridge, Hackett Publishing Company, 1998, 117- 120.

[8] Radhakrishnan and P.T. Raju. *The Concept Of Man: The Concept of Man in Greek Thought*, New Delhi, Harper Collins Publishers India, 1997, 43.

The faculty of intellect facilitates the act of reflection, memory and imagination as mentioned earlier. On the other hand, the faculty of will is very crucial in human conduct. The will is always directed towards what is good. Human intellect and will are inseparable and they complement each other. Immanuel Kant in his treatise, The Critique of Pure Reason remarks that "we are not merely minded entities involving in the just perceiving, judging and theorizing, rather we are agents, we do things and we affect the world by our actions as well as being affected by the world in perception." [9]

In this respect too we transcend the animals and other entities of the world. Since animals cannot give reasons for their actions and behaviour they cannot really said to have rationality in them. In this sense they do not act, they only behave in a particular manner. Today our libraries and universities are filled with books and research papers that elucidate the dissimilarities between human being and other animals. Daniel J. Sullivan states, the uniqueness of human person in his book:

> Besides being an animal, man has a
> power - the power of reason which in itself
> makes him different in kind from the rest of
> the universe. Man can see the sameness in
> difference which runs through things, the

---

[9] Stevenson Leslie and D.L Haberman, *Ten Theories of Human Nature,* New York, Oxford University Press, 1998, 117.

ones in many, and the enduring reality behind outward change. Man knows meaning and law and purpose and, through his power of free choice, he can choose between various alternatives, which are presented to him by his intellect. In short, man is a being altogether unique as compared with the rest of the physical universe, because in knowing and judging he rises above the inexorable law and rigidity of the realm of matter[10]

As Sullivan has noted man is not merely material being, for he rises above the material realm. But, for empiricists and scientists, man is a material being, and is subject to the laws of nature. Furthermore, they add that man is deeply immersed in the impersonal forces of physical universe and also display many traits in common with the animals.

However, when it comes to the comparison of the activities, for instance: arts and the sciences, the ordering of oneself and society, for which there is no parallel in the animal world. The distinction between the rational and free activities of man and purely animal activities are so great, that the similarities are insignificant in comparison. Thus it

---

[10] Daniel J. Sullivan, *An Introduction to Philosophy*, New York, The Bruce Publishing Company, 1957, 57.

is obvious that, man is a different kind of being in the universe because of his abstract reasoning.[11]

Thus man is not just a being reducible to cosmological matter of this world, but a transient being, a subject rather an object, who has the capacity to go beyond. Nevertheless, for the most part throughout history, man was not given the proper significance, the dignity and respect of his being, was just considered as one of the beings, an object in the world. As we have seen above with his unique rational nature he is always something more than other creatures in the world. Further he deserves a different term to call himself other than man. Hitherto the most appropriate term to address man is: human person.

1.3. Man as a human person

To have a proper understanding of the human being as a human person, it is noteworthy to differentiate the distinction between the concept of 'man' and 'human person.' These two concepts are essentially different but they complement each other. The former concept addresses human being as being in the world in a cosmological view. On the other hand, the latter understands human being inwardly. This concept of human person gives rise to human being's innerness, uniqueness and irreducible character as person in the world. In defining human being as a human person, the term

---

[11] Sullivan, *An Introduction to Philosophy*, 58.

'person' also has a special character. The word 'person' originally derives from a Latin term 'persona'. And its etymological meaning describes an actor or a performer, who wears a mask in a drama. In those stage plays actors used a mask to hide their identity in order to act their parts well. In another sense this word '*per*' means 'through', while '*sonare*' means 'sound,' therefore, '*personare*' means to speak through.[12]

In the medieval era this particular word 'person' earned a new notion with the Christian culture. This new concept of person emphasized the individuality and the uniqueness of the person leading to one's dignity. Among the thinkers who gave philosophical definition to this concept, Augustine, comes first in order. Basically, he was involved in attempting to grasp the meaning of the concept 'person' in connection with the theory of Holy Trinity. He understood human person as an individual and a single entity. The successor of Augustine was Severus Boethius. For Boethius, "a person is an individual substance of rational nature."[13] Later, Thomas Aquinas gives an ontological definition to 'person' referring to it as an integral and unitary self-subsistent subject, characterized by intellectual consciousness, moral

---

[12] Anthony Flew, "*Person*" in, A Dictionary of Philosophy, London: Pan Books Ltd.,1984.265.
[13] Thomas Aquinas, *Summa Theologiae* II-I, Q 29, Art. 2, (Reply 5), 311.

freedom and all properties that ensure from these qualities. [14]

With the beginning of the industrial revolution there was a tendency to deny the uniqueness, the absolute value and the sacredness of the individual. And this tendency became a reality both in ninetieth and twentieth centuries. In other words, this era was marked out by the destruction brought against the human person in both thought and in practice. In thought, the destruction was brought by reductionist and nihilistic approaches towards human life and dignity. In practice the destruction of human person was caused by the genocide, the deliberate murder of over hundred million innocent people in the world wars. In addition to this, the value of human life was ruined in practice by legal and illegal abortions, euthanasia; and innumerable instances of immoral behaviours.

Fortunately, in this era a group of great thinkers under the leadership of Emmanuel Mounier stood against all these destructive forms of life, together with Max Scheller, Martin Buber, Levinas and Karol Wojtyla. They developed a new line of thought against individualism and subjectivism namely, personalism.(this particular concept is developed in the third chapter with more details). They considered 'human person' as an incarnated

---

[14] Aquinas, *Summa Theologiae* II-I,Q 29 Art. 2, (Objection 5), 311.

existence. Furthermore, their concept was based on inter-subjective nature which was later developed by Martin Buber. Buber in his treatise, *I and Thou* renders most of the relevant instances with regard to the basic types of relationships that human person builds and has with things and persons. Thus in his writings he exhorts us to consider the other as a 'human person' but not as a thing or and object. [15]

As we have seen above, the concept of man as a 'human person' is more accurate when he is addressed as a concrete individual with the rational nature through which his personal subjectivity is realized. From his corporeal dimension he is an individual, who is subjected to the laws of nature. From his spiritual dimension he escapes the laws of matter, and becomes a being that self-knows, with eternal destiny, a human person. Consequently, his unique nature urges him to reflect and question everything that he experiences, even the mere fact of his own existence, the reason for his existence and the meaning of his life. In this reflection he is often confronted with his conduct, the conduct which is composed of different activities that he performs.[16] Therefore, it is apt to consider his moral nature in the following subheading.

---

[15] William R. Schroeder, *Continental Philosophy, a Critical Approach,* Oxford, Blackwell Publishers, 2005, 228 - 229.
[16] Roland B. Fransisco, *Karol Wojtyla's Theory of Participation: Based on His Christian Personalism*, Manila, St. Paul's Publications, 1995, 13.

2. Moral nature of human person

As the whole human life span appears to be a chain of actions, in each human person there arises a quest to know, if his acts give any meaning to his life. Human person not only look at his own acts, but also of others' acts, for their acts have impacts on him. Thus, it is vital to consider the moral nature and the ethical behaviour of human person, when analysing his quest for meaning in life.

2.1. Freedom of choice

When analysing his quest for meaning in life. Human freewill is another outstanding feature of the human essence that characterizes human person from the animal kingdom. Through this feature human person experiences himself as an active agent in the universe, who determines his action and ultimately his own destiny.

Therefore, he becomes not just a being in the world but a 'being at the world,' who is self-conscious, an active agent.[17]

On the other hand, when it comes to non-human beings specifically animals, their instinct plays a major in their behaviour. Basically, their behaviour

---

[17] Jean L. Mercier, *Being Human,* Bangalore: Asian Trading Cooperation, 1998, 60.

is controlled and guided by their predetermined nature; hence they lack freewill.[18] Human will is generally drawn towards what is good, good in the universal sense by the power of intellect. Nevertheless, this universal good is unable to confront by human persons because of their finiteness. Therefore, what human persons confront is mere finite and limited good. Thus, a human person uses his free will to choose between finite good and universal good in this material universe.[19]

Moreover, man's freedom to act or not to act is considered as a presupposition of his moral responsibility.[20] Freewill cannot be blamed, for it is the intellect which guides the will. Hence it is wrong to state that the will chooses the alternatives rather it is man, who chooses by means of his freewill.[21] For instance, if the intellect embraces wealth, pleasure and power in their extreme sense, instead of virtues, for the fulfilment in life, for certain, the intellect is deceived through false knowledge.[22] According to the preceding facts, the right use of intellect in guiding our free will matters a lot in quest purpose and meaning in life.

---

[18] *Mercier, Being Human, 62.*
[19] Ibid., 95.
[20] Harold H. Titus, *Ethics for Today*, 3rd ed., New Delhi, Eurasia Publishing House Private Limited, 1996, 93.
[21] Edwin Savundar, *The Philosophy of Form and Human Person*, New York, Wisdom Publications, 2004, 81.
[22] Ibid.

In the course of history we find sublime life examples, for those who used their intellect and free will in a proper manner. Among them, in the philosophical circle, Socrates preferred to die than to undergo injustice.[23] On the contrary, there are also persons who misused free will and contributed for the destruction of human society in the history of human civilization, for instance, the dictators such as Hitler and Stalin. Thus, through these instances we can see how these men have utilized their free will to determine the meaning of their lives.

2.2. Human acts and their morality

As I have mentioned earlier, our life appears to be a chain of actions. These actions in general, fall into two categories, namely acts of man and human acts. All actions do not fall into the subject matter of ethics and moral conduct of human persons.[24] Therefore, first of all, a comprehensive explanation on the human acts and the acts of man will clear out our doubts. Thomas Aquinas in his celebrated masterpiece, Summa Theologiae defines human actions as follows:

> Of actions done by man those alone are properly called human which are proper to man as man. Now man differs from irrational

---

[23] Sullivan, *An Introduction Philosophy,* 101.
[24] Kandakavil Thomas, *Ethical World, A Study on the Ethical Thought in the West and the East*, Banglore, Darmaram Publications, 1995, 166.

animals in this that he is the master of his actions. Wherefore those actions alone are properly called human, of which man is master. Now man is the master of his actions through his reason and will, whence too the free will is defined as faculty of will and reason. Therefore, those actions are properly called human which proceed from a deliberate will. And if any actions are found in man, they can be called actions of man, but not properly human actions, since they are not proper to man as man.[25]

According to Aquinas, an act becomes human in so far as it proceeds from a deliberated will of a person. Every person possesses the gift of freedom to act, or in a specific sense the free will to act in any given situation. Furthermore, his actions in collections are called, conduct. Through this conduct, his character is identified in the society as good or bad person. Man as a human person performs actions proper to his nature both freely and consciously. On the other hand, the actions that flow from the spontaneous reactions of the will are 'acts of man.' Examples are breathing, eye blinks, and food digestion. They happen without our knowledge and freewill. Therefore, we are not masters of these actions.[26]

---

[25] Thomas Aquinas, *Summa Theologiae*, I-II, Q1, Art. 1, (Answer), 4.
[26] Thomas, *Ethical World,* 167.

In brief, it's only the man whose action flows from the will directed by the reason. Thus, it is commonly said that human action is always conscious and freely willed. Consequently, what is not conscious and freely willed is not an action of man as man; it is not a human action, although it takes place in man. Now of all actions, human acts are of our concern in this research. They alone constitute the subject matter of ethics. Moreover, they are inseparable from the fact of man's existence as man. Now it is very clear that the human will of man is ultimately manifested through his actions.

All religions speak much on proper moral and ethical behaviour of the human person. For instance, the Catholic Church defines the human acts as: "acts that are freely chosen in consequence of a judgment of conscious."[27] John Paul II in his apostolic letter, Veritatis Splendor exhorts on the morality of human acting this way, "The morality of the human act depends primarily and fundamentally on the 'Object' rationally chosen by the deliberated will..."[28] Here, he stresses that acting is morally good when the choices of freedom are in conformity with man's true good. Furthermore, according to the Catechism of the Catholic Church, "the object, the intention and the circumstances

---

[27] *Catechism of the Catholic Church*, New Delhi, Theological Publications India, 1994, 1749.
[28] John Paul II, Veritatis *Splendor*, The Modern World and Contemporary Moral Theology, Vatican City, Liberia Editrice Vaticana, 1996, 78.

make up the source or constitute elements of the morality of human acts."[29] Thus it is clear that the moral value of human acts depends above all on the conformity of the object willed by one's reason. Therefore, as it is mentioned earlier, if one's 'will' is directed towards objects that are incapable being ordered to good it turns to be intrinsically evil acts, which are against the promotion of life. The Second Vatican Council specifies several examples of intrinsically evil inhuman acts in the pastoral constitutions of the Church in the modern world:

Any type of murder, genocide, abortion, euthanasia or wilful self-destruction, whatever violates the integrity of the human person, such as mutilation, torments inflicted on body or mind, attempts to coerce the will itself; whatever insult human dignity, such as subhuman living condition, arbitrary imprisonment, deportation, slavery, prostitution, the selling women and children; as well as disgraceful working conditions, where men are treated as mere tools for profit, rather than as free and responsible persons; all these things and others of their like are infamies indeed...[30]

According to the teachings of the Catholic Church, the morality of human acts depends on our intentions. In all human activities intention appears

---

[29]*Catechism of the Catholic Church*, 1750.
[30] *Second Vatican council*, Gaudium et Spes, the Pastoral Constitution of the Church in the Modern World, ed. Austin Flannery, Vatican Council II, Bombay, St. Paul Publications, 1975, 27.

to be the movement of the will towards the end. It is very clear in the words of Catechism of the Catholic Church: "It even can orient one's life towards its ultimate end..."[31]

Now having discussed the difference between acts of man and human acts, and the moral responsibility of our deliberate acts, we see every rational being does act in order to attain some satisfaction and fulfilment in life. Thus, it is due to the quest for the ultimate good in him. This quest will last until his death, and in this life journey one can choose to do good acts or bad acts habitually. Eventually these habits show us whether one is striving to live a virtuous life or wretched life.[32]

In the inquiry of man's quest for meaning in life, we have analysed previously his freedom to act, human conduct and the morality of human acts. Now we shall turn to man's orientation towards virtuous life primarily focusing on the teachings of Aristotle and Aquinas. As it is mentioned above, man's will is always directed towards what is good, and this goodness can only be found if he leads a virtuous life.

---

[31] *Catechism of the Catholic Church, 1752.*
[32] Aristotle, *The Nicomachean Ethics*, Aristotle's Ethics, tr. in English J.A. K. Thomson, London, Penguin Books Ltd., 1955, 2, 7-12.

2.3. Man's orientation towards a virtuous life

Aristotle and many other virtue ethicists affirm that by our nature we are drawn towards a purpose and our potential to achieve good. Moreover, they specify and stress upon the importance of virtue, in attaining both moral wellbeing and inner harmony.[33]

Aristotle, in Nicomachean Ethics speaks of a particular kind of inner harmony, which he calls 'eudemonia.' Here, 'eudemonia' should not be confused with what utilitarian and egoists call 'happiness.' It is rather a kind of fulfilment and good we 'quest' for by our nature as human beings. In a way it is similar to the notion of the eastern and modern western concepts such as spiritual enlightenment, nirvana and self-actualization. .[34]

Although Aristotle specified, that human beings have a natural inclination to be virtuous, later he adds that: "the moral virtues, then, are produced in us neither by nature nor against nature. Nature, indeed, prepares us the ground for their reception, but their complete formation is the product of habit."[35] Thus, it is very clear that moral virtue is

---

[33] Judith A. Boss, *Ethics for Life*, London, Mayfield Publication Company, 1998, 392.
[34] *Ibid., 388.*
[35] Aristotle, *The Nicomachean Ethics, 2, 1.*

the outcome of habit rather than a product of our natural endowments.

Moreover, according to Aristotle "virtue is that which makes its possessor good and his work good likewise."[36] Again, for Aristotle an act is virtuous in so far as it maintains itself in the 'mean' which avoids the excess of too much and too little. Because excess is possible in either direction, there are two vices corresponding to two virtues.[37] For instance, in the case of courage, there may be excess of courage as foolhardiness, or there may be deficiency of courage as cowardice.[38] Now turning to the definition of Aquinas, "virtue is a good quality or a habit of the rational powers which renders them capable of acting rightly, and which cannot be used badly."[39] According to him virtue signifies the perfection of human nature, and vices degrading of the human nature.

Throughout the history and in many religions, those who lived virtuous lives have been recognized as exemplary personages, or in other words, as saints. For instance, in Confucianism, saintliness was a state of ethical perfection best exemplified in holy leaders of primeval times. Mahayana Buddhism views all people having the potentiality to attain Buddhahood, thus, of sainthood. On the other hand,

---

[36] Aristotle, The Nicomachean Ethics, 2, 5.
[37] Ibid, 2, 6.
[38] Ibid., 2, 7.
[39] Thomas Aquinas, *Summa Theologiae, I-II, Q55, Art. 4, (Answer), 448.*

in Theravada Buddhism, all disciples of the Buddha, who attained Nirvana, were called 'Arahath'. This term 'Arahat' is roughly equal to the English word 'saint.' [40]

In Christianity the connotation of the word 'saint' is dense in meaning. It is more than the morally exemplary life one lives. For instance, to mention some of the salient characteristics of a saint according to Pope Benedict XIV are as follows. First of all, a saint finds abundant joy in doing his duty and in suffering greatly for the love of God. Then he or she performs virtuous acts whenever occasion calls for them. Finally virtuous acts are done promptly and with certain ease. [41]

Moreover, as all religions speak on the importance of virtues in one way or another, Christianity, in particular, in her teachings defines it in this manner: "The human virtues are stable dispositions of the intellect and the will that govern our acts, order our passions, and guide our conduct in accordance with reason and faith. They can be grouped around the four cardinal virtues, prudence, justice, fortitude, and temperance." [42]

---

[40] Georges Paul, "Philosophical Anthropology" in, *Encyclopedia Britannica,* Vol.17, 435.

[41] Thomas E. Dubay, "Saint," in, *The Catholic Encyclopedia for Schools and Homes*, Vol. 9, New York, McGraw-Hill Publishers, 1965, 538 – 540.

[42] *Catechism of the Catholic Church*, 1834.

In line with this one of the classical examples for a saint, who is distinguished by these virtues, in particular for temperance, is Francis of Assisi. Who lived a very simple exemplary virtuous life, many began to love the way he lived and joined him. Not only him, there are many more exemplary personages in diverse walks of life. For example, another type of saintliness is reflected in the person of Indian leader and reformer, Mahatma Gandhi. As a reformer he devoted his whole life to acquire political freedom for his country. He also lived a kind of a virtuous life characterized by these ideals. First among them is Satyagraha: holding fast to the truth with all the powers of the spirit. Secondly, ahimsa: the method of non-violence and lastly, brahmahcaraya: the ascetic way of life. [43]

These life examples make us clear, that although human person has an orientation within him towards a virtuous life, he chooses to live it to the degree he wants. This could be due to lack of knowledge he possesses about his human nature. If our knowledge had been perfect, our passions and acts would have been under the full control of our reason.

Since our finite knowledge is imperfect our control over passions is also not perfect. As a result of this

---

[43] Robert L. Holmes, "Gandhi, Mohandas Karaenchand," *The Cambridge Dictionary of Philosophy*, gen. ed. Robert Audi, New York, Cambridge University Press, 1995, 293.

we tend to form habits that do not contribute to the perfection of our nature as man as a human person. Yet, it is also obvious that people make an attempt in their life to attain knowledge in order to discover them and to know the truth of their lives. This leads us to the next chapter, which will discuss the never-ending quest for genuine knowledge and truth in human person.

Chapter Two

THE 'QUEST' FOR KNOWLEDGE AND THE TRUTH

The second chapter is devoted to inquiring man's 'quest' for genuine knowledge and truth in view of interpreting meaning to human life. Man with his 'quest' journeying towards the ultimate meaning realizes that many sources of knowledge are deceptive and are meaningless. Thus, in this chapter, the 'quest' for knowledge in the history, the sources of knowledge and the theories of knowledge will be discussed under the first subheading. Then the second subheading will make an inquiry on the 'quest' for the true knowledge, examining man's desire for truth and the theories of truth.

1. The Thirst for knowledge

Every human person struggles with the 'quest' for meaning in life.[44] In everyday life he is riddled with anxiety to discover solutions to complex and complicated problems, for his life appears to be absurd. On one hand, man possesses an unlimited urge for scaling the loftiest heights of ambition and of attaining the pinnacle of perfection in the diverse domains of his activity. On the other hand, his limitations exist to such an extent that he is simply incapable of determining the ultimate consequences of his actions with any amount of certainty.[45] Yet, with all that he finds universe too vast for his tiny, brilliant, brain. The more he advances in his 'quest' for knowledge, the more he becomes convinced of the infiniteness of the expanse of reality. His discovery of a new fact is at the same time a discovery of the truth that there exist numberless unknown facts yet to be discovered. However, this thirst for knowledge is never satisfied.[46]

One of the fundamental facts about human being is his ability to know about things around him, things beyond him, and above all about himself. Aristotle begins his book, Metaphysics with these

---

[44] Viktor Frankl, *Man's Search for Meaning in Life,* tr. in English, Ilse Lasch, New York, Washington Square Press, 1959, 172.

[45] Irving Singer, *Meaning in Life: The Harmony of Nature and Spirit*, Vol. 1, London, The Mit press, 2010, 13.

[46] Ibid., 148.

words "by nature all men long to know." [47]   Kant raises the question 'what can I know?' in the Critique of Pure Reason.[48]   Thus it is clear that our drive to know is fundamental to being a human person. According to Aristotle, this desire to know springs from our rational nature. Moreover, it has led us to unravel the mysteries of the universe through scientific experimentations. On the other hand in philosophical level this 'quest' had led us to engage in deep thinking. Attempting to discover the answers to following questions: what are the means by which our knowledge is acquired? What is the extent of our knowledge, and what are the standards or criteria by which we can judge the reliability of knowledge.

1.1 The thirst for knowledge in the history

In the cause of history, it was the ancient Greek philosophers who were concerned with the questions of validity of human knowledge. For instance, Heraclitus believed in the reliability of senses and change; in fact he held that everything is in flux, and therefore that our intellectual

---

[47] Aristotle, *The Metaphysics*, tr. in English and ed., Hugh Lawson, London, Penguin Books Ltd., 2004, 980a.
[48] Norman Kemp, *A Commentary to Kant's Critique of Pure Reason,* New York, Palgrave Macmillan Ltd., 2003, 17.

knowledge is a falsification of changing reality. [49] Parmenides in contrast denied the validity of human knowledge, claiming that everything is actually one thing, which is 'Being'. For him everything is known through the one, universal concept of 'Being'.[50] Then appeared the Sophists, who despaired of certainty altogether in pursuit of knowledge. With the beginning of new era, Socrates, Plato and Aristotle vindicated human knowledge, stressing the importance of the universal concept through which the human mind represents the various aspects of reality to itself. Socrates in particular, as Bertrand Russell writes in his history of western philosophy:

> … consistently maintains that he knows nothing, and is only wiser than others in knowing that he knows nothing; but he does not think knowledge unobtainable. On the contrary, he thinks the search for knowledge of the utmost importance. He maintains that no man sins wittingly and therefore only knowledge is needed to make all men perfectly virtuous.[51]

Moreover, another popular dictum attributed to Socrates concerning knowledge is 'know thy self'. Plato also, in line with Socrates stated the importance of knowledge to be a 'philosopher king.'

---

[49] Bertrand Russell, *A History Western Philosophy*, London, George Allen and Unwin Brothers Ltd, 1947, 62.
[50] Ibid., 67.
[51] Russell, *A History Western Philosophy*, 111.

His famous allegory of the cave exhibits his theory of knowledge. [52] Aristotle also in his Nicomachean Ethics stated that, excellence of knowledge will lead to true practice of virtue.[53] In the Middle Ages, with the rise and the spread of Christianity the 'quest' for true knowledge had a different orientation. Most of the Christian Philosophers opposed to sceptics considered, human knowledge as a divine revelation based on the faith. In this regard Augustine driven by his lifelong 'quest' for wisdom and true knowledge engaged in philosophical 'quest' to find the intellectual certainty. At first, misled by sceptics, he held that the truth cannot be comprehended by men.[54]   But latter, after his conversion he stated the possibility of attaining intellectual certainty through his theory of illumination, placing faith before reason. For Augustine, the highest mode of knowledge was the knowledge of God. It is very clear when he wrote in his Confession: "Oh God thou hast created us for

---

[52] Sparshott F.E., *"Plato as a Political Thinker"*, Plato: A Biography of His Visions and Ideas, ed. Subrata Mukherjee and Sushila Ramaswamy, New Delhi, Deep and Deep Publications, 1998, 396.
[53] Hamlyn D.W., *"Aristotle on Dialectics"*, Aristotle: A Biography of His Visions and Ideas, ed. Subrata Mukherjee and Sushila Ramaswamy, New Delhi, Deep and Deep Publications, 1998, 592-593.
[54] Samuel Enoch Stumpf, *Philosophy: History and Problems*, 5th ed., New York, McGraw- hill Publications, 1994, 136.

thyself so that our hearts are restless until they find their rest in thee." [55]

After Augustine, the most prominent Christian philosopher is Thomas Aquinas, who left us a huge literary legacy. Aquinas in his 'quest' for knowledge followed the footsteps of Aristotle. He disputed against Plato and his followers stating that human mind knows what it does through its confrontation with actual concrete objects. Moreover, he claimed that our mind is able to grasp universal in the particulars and our human mind does not possess any innate ideas but rather it has the potentiality to attain knowledge. Standing by Aristotle, Thomas stated that there could be no knowledge without sense experience.[56]

At the beginning of sixteen century, new emphasis was placed on human knowledge by Francis Bacon. He wanted to reconstruct the sciences, arts and all human knowledge because, in his day, the 'quest' for knowledge was reduced only to studying ancient texts and ability to quote ancient philosophers. Bacon disagreed with this kind of out-dated learning, emphasizing the importance of utility of knowledge.[57] Another renowned philosopher, Descartes, sought just one principle from which he could conclude that all knowledge is deduced as

---

[55] Augustine, *The Confessions* tr. in English, Tobie Matthew, ed., Roder Huddleston, London, Fontana Books, 1963. I,1,
[56] Stumpf, *Philosophy*, 195.
[57] Russell, *A History Western Philosophy*, 564 -567.

theorems in Geometry.[58] The modern period marks the pinnacle of epistemological investigation to find the criteria to discover the real truth up until the contemporary philosophers take charge. Up to now, we have come a long way from the Pre Socratics to modern philosophers unravelling the 'quest' for true knowledge in the history of mankind. This 'quest' did not, in fact stop with the modern period, it still continues.

1.2 The sources of knowledge

Knowledge leading to true knowledge is very crucial in the journey towards finding meaning of human life. Philosophers from antiquity have wondered where this knowledge ultimately comes from and what source of knowledge is the best to be trusted. In the world there are many ways and means to gain knowledge, but all the sources are not as reliable or accurate as we might desire. Thus, it is vital to analyse some of the basic sources of knowledge in order to identify the sources that offer greater reliability to find truth. From an epistemological basis the sources of knowledge can be divided into two major types: namely primary sources and secondary sources. The basic primary sources include sense perception and intellection, while the secondary sources include; testimony,

---

[58] Russell, *A History Western Philosophy*, 586.

intuition and mystical knowledge and indirect knowledge.[59]

First of all, consider the relevance of sense perception, which is one of the basic primary sources. Although, all knowledge does not arise from sense perception it is the ultimate ground of all knowledge. In other words, all other sources of knowledge presuppose perception.[60] Sense perception includes five major ways in which we perceive the reality with our sense organs. They are sight, sound, odour, taste and touch.[61] The essential character of perception is the contact between senses and the object of perception. Internal contents of human cognition like pain, pleasure etc. are cognized through mind and is called mental perception.[62] However, on the issue of the relevance and accuracy of the sense perception, there are on-going debates. The main weakness of the sense perception is its deceptiveness.[63] It can, at times, deceive us since objects given to the senses are always changing and fleeting, because our vision can play tricks. Nevertheless, philosophers have

---

[59] Avrum Stroll, *"Epistemology"* in, Encyclopaedia Britannica, Vol.18, 466.

[60] Stroll, "Epistemology" in, *Encyclopaedia Britannica,* Vol.18, 467.

[61] Bertrand Russell, *The Problems of Philosophy*, New Delhi, Oxford University Press, 2003, 4.

[62] Jonathan L. Kvanvig, *The Value of Knowledge and the Pursuit of Understanding,* New York, Cambridge University Press, 2003, 39.

[63] Ibid., 67.

stated that senses just present objects as they appear. Thus, one cannot blame sense organs for deceptive knowledge.[64] Second primary source is intellection. As we have discussed above, all knowledge is not derived from sense experience alone. Thus, some knowledge is derived from reason via intellection. Through our rationality intellection is made possible.[65]

Now turning towards the secondary sources of knowledge, let us first look at the testimony. Testimony is an important source of knowledge. Our experience shows that the major part of a person's stock of knowledge about the world is acquired from the oral or written testimony of other persons. The importance of testimony becomes obvious when we imagine a person deprived of all contact with other persons and books in which case he would simply be reduced to the level of a brute or a beast. However, when considering the relevance and validity of any testimony many questions are raised on their implausibility by philosophers and psychologists.[66] The second secondary way of attaining knowledge is through intuition. Through intuition we gain knowledge of something without being consciously aware of

---

[64] Stroll, *"Epistemology" in, Encyclopaedia Britannica, Vol.18, 466 - 467.*
[65] Moritz Schick, *General Theory of Knowledge*, tr. in English, E. Blumberg, New York, Herbert Hansberger Publication, 1974, 20-23.
[66] Kvanvig, *The Value of Knowledge, 166.*

where the knowledge came from. Carl Jung and his followers give the word 'intuition' a great variety of different meanings, ranging from direct access to unconscious knowledge, unconscious cognition, inner sensing, and the ability to understand something instinctively, without the need for conscious reasoning.[67] Descartes in his book, *Meditations on First Philosophy* refers to 'intuition' as a pre-existing knowledge gained through rational reasoning or discovering truth through contemplation.[68] Immanuel Kant finds intuition as basic sensory information provided by the cognitive faculty of sensibility. On the relevance of intuition scientists have a cheap belief, since it does not fall under observation and verification.[69]

Another secondary source of knowledge in our inquiry is the knowledge attained via mystical experience. Mystical experience is frequently defined as an experience of direct communion with God, or union with the Absolute.[70] Grounded on mystical experience, mysticism became a

---

[67] *Anthony Stevens, On Jung, London, Rutledge Publishers, 1990, 196.*

[68] Rene Descartes, *Meditations on the First Philosophy*, tr. in English and revised by Deena Weinberg, New York, BN Publishers, 2007, 87

[69] *Bruce Russell, "Intuition" in,* The Cambridge Dictionary of Philosophy, gen. ed. Robert Audi, New York, Cambridge University press, 1995, 382.

[70] *Hilda Graff, "Mystical Knowledge" in,* The Catholic Encyclopaedia for Schools and Homes, Vol. 7, Thomas E. Dubay, New York, McGraw-Hill Publishers, 1965, 411 – 412.

phenomenon found in all major religions. Those who had mystical knowledge have attained them in diverse states, such as visions, trances, levitations, locutions, raptures, and ecstasies. Teresa of Avila's ecstasies are famous examples of such mystical phenomena. But some mystics such as, Origen, Meister Chart, and John of the Cross did not have any psycho-physical phenomena when receiving mystical knowledge. However, mystics considered these states as by-products of, or accessories to, the full mystical experiences. What they valued most was the knowledge they gain through them, especially knowledge on God and Evil, Heaven and Hell.[71] However our concern here is how far we can rely on the mystical acquaintance as a source of knowledge. For instance, logical positivists held a very strong belief as not to consider this source as one of the reliable sources of knowledge.[72] Nevertheless, various philosophers and thinkers basing on some of these sources continued their 'quest' in finding theories in the light of attaining true knowledge.

1.3 The theories of knowledge

All through the history people from time to time have wondered and questioned the knowledge of

---

[71] Hilda Graff, *"Mystical Knowledge"* in, The Catholic Encyclopaedia for Schools and Homes, Vol. 7, Thomas E. Dubay, New York, McGraw-Hill Publishers, 1965, 411 – 412.
[72] Russell, *"Intuition" in, The Cambridge Dictionary of Philosophy*, 445 - 446.

basic realities namely, world, man, and God. Every generation has tried to understand these realities taking diverse approaches. Some gave more emphasis to experience and experimentation, while others gave precedence to rationalization. Moreover, another group of thinkers remained interested only on ideas, whereas others believed in 'real' reality opposing the ideas of their adversaries. Besides, there was another unique group of thinkers doubting even the fact of the possibility of attaining knowledge. Later these groups of thinkers were identified as empiricists, rationalists, idealists, realists, and sceptics respectively. However, all these attempts in pursuit of knowledge manifest the insatiable 'quest' of man to understand his place in the world.

Before introducing these theories, it is apt to consider how important they are in our day-to-day living. For example, in ordinary life do we really need to experience something in order to know it? Or can we neglect the fact of experience in knowing something? In agreement with these, does a youngster need to smoke a cigar in order to know what a cigar is? Or can we know the pain of a wounded patient as he feels it. Extreme empiricists, who emphasize the role of experience, observation and evidence, especially sensory perception in formulation of ideas and the acquisition of knowledge, would answer that we need to go through such experiences to know something which we did not know earlier, for they do not believe in any of a priori or innate knowledge.[73]

This theory of empiricism runs back to the time of Aristotle. He emphasised the importance of experience in his writings. He considered experience as the basis of knowledge.[74] In line with this, he identified our intellect as an empty sheet before encountering any experience. This is very clear when he wrote: "...that the intellect is in a way potentially the object of thoughts, but nothing in actuality before it thinks, and the potentiality is like that of the tablet on which there is nothing actually written. Just the same happens in the case of the intellect."[75] At the same time he stated that genuine knowledge does not consists in mere acquaintance with facts; it is rather concerned with their reason and causes too. In other words, gaining knowledge is impossible without experience, but to have genuine knowledge one has to purify it by reason.

In the 11th century Persian philosopher, Avicenna popularized empiricism with the concept of '*tabula rasa*' which was developed by Aristotle in his book *De Anima*. Avicenna further argued that

---

[73] Russell, "*Empiricism*" in, The Cambridge Dictionary of Philosophy, 224 - 225.
[74] Frederick Copleston, *A History of Philosophy*, Vol. 1, Greece and Rome; From the Pre-Socratic to Plotinus, New York, Bantam Doubleday publishers, 1993, 125.
[75] Aristotle, *De Anima*, tr. in English, Hugh Lawson, London, Penguin Books ltd., 1986, 203.

knowledge is gained through empirical familiarity with the objects of the world. According to him we abstract the universal concepts and further develop it through a syllogistic method of reasoning. In the Middle Ages obviously, majority of the Christian philosophers were empiricists. For example, a notable thinker in the 14th century was William Ockham, who argued that all knowledge of physical world is attained by sensory means.[76] In 16th century another English empiricist, Francis Bacon believed in building up observed information about nature so as to arrive at an accurate picture of the world. Later, with the appearance of Locke's Essay, the doctrine of Empiricism was first explicitly formulated. In his book *"A Essay Concerning Human Understanding"* he argued that the mind is a 'blank slate' on which experience leaves marks and therefore denied that humans have innate ideas. Consequently in his argument there arose a problem concerning God, because we cannot perceive God as we perceive material objects. Therefore, he held that some knowledge could be attained through intuition as well.[77]

The Irish Bishop, George Berkeley saw that Locke's view could lead to atheism. So, in his

---

[76] Frederick Copleston, *A History of Philosophy*, Vol. 3, Late Medieval and Renaissance Philosophy, New York, Bantam Doubleday Publishers, 1993, 64.

[77] Frederick Copleston, *A History of Philosophy*, Vol. 5, Modern philosophy: The British Philosophers from Hobbes to Hume, New York, Bantam Doubleday publishers, 1993, 108-109.

treatise he argued that things only exist either as a result of their being perceived or by virtue of the fact that it is an entity engage in perceiving.[78] Another Empiricist philosopher David Hume in his inquiry concerning human understanding disputed that all human knowledge can be divided into two categories: relation of ideas (contingent observation of the world), and matters of facts (mathematics and logic). He asserted that ideas are derived from our sensations or impressions.[79] Furthermore according to him, our present sensations depend on past sensations and, consequently, we can infer future sensations from the present. Thus, this shows that there is no absolute certainty in knowledge in his point of view. Taking everything into account, the theory of empiricism holds that experience, observation and evidence, especially sensory perception is vital in formulation of ideas and the acquisition of knowledge, while rejecting the role of innate and a priori knowledge.

The theory of rationalism is the contrast of the prior theory. The prominent rationalist, namely Descartes, Spinoza and Leibniz picked up the ideas of early Greek philosophers who stressed the importance of reason as the origin of knowledge.[80] Among them Descartes was inspired by the

---

[78] Raj Bali, *Introduction to Philosophy*, 2 ed., New Delhi, Sterling Publishers, 1997, 58.

[79] Copleston, *A History of Philosophy*, Vol. 5, 263.

[80] Russell, "*Rationalism*" in, The Cambridge Dictionary of Philosophy, 673- 675.

mathematical certainty of modern science and wanted to find the same certainty in other areas of knowledge. [81] In brief those who embrace this theory consider reason as the natural source of knowledge. Moreover they believed that reason which is successful at mathematics and sciences can also be transferred to any field to find the truth. Hence the true knowledge is not attained through senses but via rationalizing. Hitherto we have seen two theories of knowledge; the next is theory of knowledge was expounded by the German philosopher, Kant.

With the arrival of Immanuel Kant, many syntheses emerged in diverse inquiries. Among them, the synthesis he provided for problem of knowledge is crucial for our discussion as a theory of knowledge. In line with the theory of Kant, knowledge is neither purely a prior nor wholly a posteriori. Thus, the formal knowledge is by reason and the material knowledge is gain by experience. Further he stated that our mind arranges these syntheses and gradually fabricate knowledge.[82] In this way our mind can grasp the material reality only as it appears to the senses. Mind or reason cannot independently apprehend the reality without the aid of experience; therefore, he stated

---

[81] Russell, "*Rationalism*" in, The Cambridge Dictionary of Philosophy, 673- 675.

[82] Georges Dicker, *Kant's Theory of Knowledge: An Analytical Introduction*, New York, Oxford University Press, 2004, 3.

that, we can know the reality only as it appears, not as it really is.[83] With this novel idea Kant placed a limit to our scope of knowledge taking a transcendental idealistic approach to answer the 'quest' for external world. This is related to the theory of idealism, which denies the existence of objects independent of human perception. Apart from mind, there can be no world of objects.[84] According to Berkley, a correct analysis shows that a material object consists of nothing but ideas, whether in the mind of God or of the conscious agents that he has created.[85]

The last but one is the theory of scepticism, which maintains the attitude that sure knowledge of how things really are may be sought, but cannot be found. Sceptics doubt almost all the sources of knowledge including the meaning of life. In a positive way, this approach creates continuous search and desire for certain knowledge. But, in the strongest sense it holds the view that by no means we are able to attain true knowledge. Opposing to sceptic's view appears the realists, who affirm the existence of realty independent of senses and mind. This appears to be the most reliable theory of knowledge in our inquiry. After having discussed the possible theories of attaining genuine

---

[83] Georges Dicker, *Kant's Theory of Knowledge: An Analytical Introduction*, New York, Oxford University Press, 2004, 7.
[84] Raj Bali, *Introduction to Philosophy*, 29.
[85] Anthony, *"Idealism" in,* Dictionary of Philosophy, 160-161.

knowledge, the next step in this inquiry is to find the ultimate Truth.

2. Man's search for the truth

Man's desire to know the ultimate truth, and to find the purpose for his being in this universe, is very clear when we look at the evolution of human knowledge in the history of thought. Moreover, every human being in one moment or the other in his life confronts the question: 'what is truth?' According to Aristotle this 'quest' for truth emerges from the depth of every human being.[86] Furthermore Aristotle states: "The investigation of the truth is in a way a difficult and in a way easy. An indication is that no one can worthily reach it nor does everyone completely miss it, but each thinker says something about nature, and individually they make small contributions to it and from them all together a certain volume arises."[87]

2.1. The desire for truth

In fact, every human being desires to know the truth in a three-dimensional way. At first he is concerned about the truth of the material world which surrounds him (world). Secondly, he is engrossed in the truth about the present human life (man). Finally, his thirst for truth is about the life

---

[86] Aristotle, *The Metaphysics*, 980a.
[87] *Ibid., 993b.*

after and the reality beyond (God). To explain these 'quests' in depth will result endless pages of inquiry; therefore, the next subheading is confined only to the epistemological answer given to the problem of truth.

2.2 Various theories of Truth

In our day-to-day living we communicate and acquire knowledge about world, man and God mostly by means of statements. These statements are verified as true statements by various theories namely, the correspondence, coherence, and pragmatic theories of truth. First, according to the correspondence theory a statement is true, if only it corresponds to the reality mentioned. For instance, when we state that 'there is a pen on the table,' that statement is true according to the correspondence theory only if, the 'pen' in question actually is on the table. Aristotle was referring to the correspondence theory of truth when he said, "Of truth in general, to say that something is when it is, is true. To say that something is when it is not is false."[88] Thomas Aquinas, following in the steps of Aristotle affirmed that, truth is the agreement or conformity of thing and intellect.[89]

A significant alternative to correspondence theory is the coherence theory, according to which

---

[88] Aristotle, *The Metaphysics*, 1062a.
[89] Stroll, "*Epistemology*," in, Encyclopaedia Britannica, Vol. 18, 466 - 467.

the truthfulness of a proposition is implicit in its 'coherence' with other propositions. Mathematics, geometry, physics, and logic are examples of coherent systems of truth. A statement is true if it coheres with a system of other statements, and false if it fails to cohere. But the coherence at issue is not coherence with reality or with facts. According to this theory a thought should develop and become more and more coherent until it is literally identical to, or one with reality. Hence reality is the realization of a fully articulated and maximally coherent system of judgments.

Next, the pragmatic theory envisages a conception of truth that recognizes a close link between truth and human experience. The pragmatic theory of truth bases itself on the intuition that one cannot profit from error either by rejecting a true proposition or by accepting a false proposition. Being right is the most advantageous policy, and so highest utility is a safe indicator of truth. The prominent advocates of classical pragmatism are Charles Peirce, William James, and John Dewey.[90]

With the arrival of postmodern thinkers, Martin to Heidegger stated that there is an absolute world structure that grounds the possibility of objective truth, and our thoughts become true when they

---

[90] Nicholas Rescher, Epistemology, *An Introduction to the Theory of Knowledge,* New York, A State University of New York Press, 2003, 43- 45.

conform to that structure.[91] It is our way of being in the world that makes truth and falsity possible. Heidegger's view challenges the idea that truth is a static, binary relation between a subject's representation of an object and that object itself.[92] Truth is neither correspondence nor coherence but the product of an activity that presents the world directly. Truth depends on humanity in some sense. "There is truth only when and as long as '*Dasein*' exists."[93] Without human thinkers there would be no true thoughts.

Moreover, this thought was supported by Etienne Gilson's notion of the 'methodical realism,' which urges us to move toward the reality in real entities rejecting representations to arrive at truth. In his book, *Methodical Realism* he mentions that "...philosophical reflection ought necessarily to go from thought to things."[94] In fact in this era, among the contemporary thinkers we notice that, they have a tendency to deal with real existential things than on focussing their attention on the theoretical hypothesises.

---

[91] Martin Heidegger, *Being and Time*, tr. in English, John Macquarie and Robinson, Oxford, Basil Blackwell Publishers Ltd., 1962, 264.
[92] Heidegger, *Being and Time*, 260.
[93] Ibid., 271.
[94] Etienne Gilson, *Methodical Realism, A Hand Book for Beginning Realists,* tr. in English, Philip Trower, San Francisco, Ignatius Press Publication, 2011, 11.

Chapter Three

POSSIBLE ANSWERS TO THE ULTIMATE QUESTION

The third chapter presents various answers to our fundamental question, "what is the meaning of life" from different perspectives. First, how various philosophical schools in modern times look at the human life are presented. Secondly, answers to the ultimate question are suggested through anthropological and religious perspectives.

1. Modern views on human life

As discussed in the preceding chapters, man's quest to know the meaning and purpose of his life arises due to his unique rational nature. No other living being is concerned with this fundamental existential question as humans. Thus, humans all through the history have attempted to answer this question taking diverse approaches. Yet there is no concrete answer to the fundamental question at hand. Centuries dated from 19th to 21st spoke more on the meaning and purpose of human person than no other time in the course of history. Moreover, no epoch in history threatened the dignity and the meaning of human life than modern times both by the influence of theories and then by practice.

Firstly, prior to the world wars, the meaning and value of human life was threatened by theories of Darwin, Marx and Freud. All of them reduced man into a mere soulless living being. For instance, ape in his evolutionary theory.[95] Marx viewed man as merely a cog in the economic state machine with materialism.[96] Finally Freud viewed man as a suppressed sex manic in his theories.[97] Secondly, human life was threatened by the most dramatic havoc, the genocide: the deliberate murder of millions of innocent people. And not just by Hitler, Stalin, and Mao, but in all so called 'free countries', where more than one and a half million human beings a year continue to be slaughtered in the womb. [98]

With this type of status quo, the dignity and the value of the human person gradually faded away and the human life appeared more and more to be meaningless. Because people, in general, were being converted and considered gradually from 'persons' to 'pronouns' from 'subject' to 'objects' form 'I' into 'It.'[99] Moreover, in this era the influence and the

---

[95] Allene Phy-Olsen. *Evolution, Creationism, and Intelligent Design,* California, Green Wood Publishers, 2010, 21.
[96] Hannah Arendt, *The Human Condition,* 2nd ed., with an introduction by Margaret Canova, London, The University of Chicago Press Ltd., 1998, 116.
[97] Brian Leister, *The Future for Philosophy*, New York, Oxford University Publication, 2006, 100.
[98] Jacob. E. Safra, "*The Genocide*" in, Encyclopaedia Britannica, Vol. 5, 183.
[99] Stump, Philosophy, 482.

impact of rational and scientific thought also caused the destruction of moral and religious value systems of the society. This was particularly caused by Nietzsche, who propagated atheism through the concept of the 'Death of God.' Using this, he wanted to bring out a new conception of human existence. The Russian writer, Dostoevsky influenced by some of the assertions of Nietzsche, envisaged in his novel, *the Brothers of Karamazov*, what would happen to people in a non-religious society, where everything is permitted.[100] All these above mentioned reasons paved the way to bring out, and revive the revolutionary existentialistic thinking into life from ancient past.

1.2 Existentialistic view

In existential thinking, human beings are individual, solitary, and free. But, in their concept, our freewill generates a deep sense of fear (*angst*) in the face of the absurdity of universe.[101] Thus it focuses on the uniqueness of each human individual as distinguished from abstract universal human qualities, to improve the condition and the quality of human life.[102]The basic foundation to this line of

---

[100] Bescherevnykh E., *The Secret of Man's Being*, Moscow, Novartis Press Agency House, 1972, 8.
[101] David Papineau, *Philosophy*: The Illustrated Guide to Understanding and Using Philosophy Today, London: Duncan Baird Publishes, 2004, 154.
[102] Walter Kaufman, *Existentialism from Dostoevsky to Sartre,* New York, The World Publishing Company, 1969, 12.

thought was laid by Danish thinker, Soren Kierkegaard in the middle of the nineteenth century. Later it was developed by Heidegger, Sartre, Jaspers, Marcel, and Simone de Beauvoir. Although they did not have a common system of existentialist philosophy, existentialist thinkers based their thinking basically on 'existence'.[103]

For Kierkegaard, the term 'existence' meant for individual human being and to exist implied being an individual, who strives, who considers alternatives, who chooses, who decides and who; above all, makes a commitment.[104] He vehemently disliked and revolted against abstract thought and traditional philosophy, in particular to Hegel's idealism. In a way, he attempted to live up to Feuerbach's admonition: "do not wish to be a philosopher in contrast to being a man...do not think as a thinker...think as a living, real being...think in existence."[105] Moreover, Kierkegaard 'to think in existence' meant to face with personal choices in any existential situation. In his writings he emphasised the value of the individual person and his subjective truth. Besides, Kierkegaard in his book, *Fear and Trembling* presents us three stages of existence: aesthetic, ethical and religious, a way to

---

[103] Papineau, *Philosophy*, 154.
[104] Mrinal Kanti, *Critical Survey of Phenomenology and Existentialism*, New Delhi, Allied Publishers Limited, 1990, 157.
[105] Stump, *Philosophy*, 483-484.

ascend towards the ultimate meaning placing our faith in God. [106]

Edmund Husserl, the father of phenomenology also contributed to the 'quest for meaning of one's life' through his phenomenological concepts. [107] In his technical and scientific language, he emphasised the act of detachment, of standing back from the realm of experienced existence in order to understand life in a proper manner. Heidegger, Merleau Ponty and Sartre were influenced by this insight of Husserl in composing their own philosophical thought.

Another philosopher who was influenced by Kierkegaard's existentialistic thought was Karl Jaspers. He saw how the subject of being and person has been obscured by the overwhelming impact of scientific thought in the contemporary mind. In all his writings he refuted that human being should be treated as a subject and not as an object. [108] Gabriel Marcel centred his philosophical thought on the problem of existence, or in other words, of our being here. He asked 'what am I?' He analysed this

---

[106] Mark Miller, *"A Three-stage Conversion in Kierkegaard's Fear and Trembling,"* Divyadaan, Vol. 28, 1, 2017,
[107] Emmanuel Levinas, *Discovering Existence with Husserl*, tr. in English and ed., Richard A. Cohen and Micheal B. Smith, Illinois, North-western University Press, 1998, 131.
[108] Kurt F. Reinhardt, *The Existentialist Revolt, The Main Themes and Phases of Existentialism*, California, The Bruce Publishing Company, 1952, 201.

question in order to answer the problem.[109] But he found unable to analyse, the word 'I' in the question since this word refers to an entity which possessed both subjective and objective aspects. Further he realized that, although human person shares a body like other objects, he is also involved in thinking as subject. He concluded that our existence is virtually irreducible form both objective and subjective aspects, for it is 'being and having'. [110] Moreover, he added that human life desires its deepest meaning from being through fidelity, in other words seeing the 'other' as a 'subject.' According to Marcel real being is discovered through real friendship and in love, where it has the power to transcend the objectivity of the other.[111]

Martin Heidegger proposed a new conception of understanding humanity and existence. Like other existential thinkers he noticed the uniqueness of our existence as human beings. He identified that only human beings unlike other beings, has a relation to their own being, because only people find themselves "thrown-into-the-world" and having chosen how to be.[112] Heidegger also stated that only human individuals undergo

---

[109] Gabriel Marcel, *Being and Having*, London, Collins Clear-Type Press Publication, 1965, 135.
[110] Paul Arthur and Lewis Edwin, *The Library of Living Philosophers,* Vol. 17, The Philosophy of Gabriel Marcel, Illinois, Open Court Publishing Company, 1991, 110 -111.
[111] Reinhardt, *The Existentialist Revolt*, 225.
[112] Heidegger, *Being and Time*, 400.

experiences of anxiety, fear, affection and a concern about death.[113]

Heidegger preferred another word for humanity in his treatise, because he perceived that in the past, the definition given to humanity was deceptive. Thus, he used the word *'Dasein'* which meant 'being there' in German. Heidegger explains this novel concept of "being-in-the-world,"[114] through our ordinary daily experiences and calls it as "average everydayness".[115] As he states in *Being and Time*, to be *'Dasein'* is to be in a different mode of being in the world. In propounding this novel concept he makes us aware that we must constantly become our true selves, or in other words, authentic, by accepting our finitude as humans. For him, we are temporal beings in this world as he writes: "we are being-towards-death".[116] Furthermore he adds our authenticity requires us to accept our unique selves with responsibility for our actions. According to Heidegger, this will lead us to find meaning to our human lives in any given situation; otherwise surely it will lead us meaninglessness and absurdity in life.[117]

---

[113] John Macquarie, *Existentialism*, New York, The World Publishing Company, 1979, 156.

[114] Heidegger, *Being and Time*, 79-80.

[115] Ibid., 69-70.

[116] Ibid., 279-278.

[117] William R. Schroeder, *Continental Philosophy, a Critical Approach*, Oxford, Blackwell Publishers, 2005, 220.

Finally, under the existentialistic view on the meaning of human life, the perspective of Jean Paul Sartre can be considered. In his approach he joined hands with Heidegger, agreeing that humans find themselves 'thrown-in-to-situations.' He asserts that purpose and meaningfulness of life are to be created by individuals.[118] Thus, as a theorist, he explored the notion of predestination, and developed his own phenomenological account of imagination as the key to the freedom of consciousness. He analysed human emotions, arguing that emotion is a freely chosen mode of relationship to the outside world. In his major philosophical work, *Being and Nothingness*, Sartre distinguished two types of consciousness. First, the consciousness 'for itself' (*pour-soi*) is free, mobile and spontaneous and self-conscious.[119] Secondly, the consciousness 'in-itself,' (*en-soi*) lacks self-consciousness, and lacks freedom.[120]

According to him consciousness is always engaged in the world of which it is conscious, and in relationships with other 'consciousnesses'. Furthermore, he adds that these relationships are 'conflictual': they are involved in a battle to maintain the position of subject and to make the other into an object. This battle is inescapable

---

[118] Jean Paul Sartre, *Being and Nothingness*, tr. in English, Hazel E. Barnes, New York, Washington Square Publication, 1956, 353-356.
[119] Sartre, *Being and Nothingness*, 404.
[120] Reinhardt, *The Existentialist Revolt*, 160-161.

according to him. Although Sartre was indeed a philosopher of freedom, his conception of freedom is often misunderstood. In *Being and Nothingness* human freedom operates against a background of facticity and situation.[121] This facticity includes all the facts about a human person which cannot be changed: my age, sex, class of origin, race and so on; my situation may be modified, but it still constitutes the starting point for change and roots consciousness firmly in the world. Here he introduces the idea of 'transcendence' to go beyond one's facticity to create meaning in life.[122]

As we have seen above, according to existentialist thinkers, unique individuals in concrete situations cannot be grasped adequately in traditional theories, and that systems of this sort conceal from us the personal task of trying to achieve self-fulfilment in our lives. Existentialists therefore start out with a detailed description of the self as an existing individual, understood as an agent involved in a specific social and historical world. One of their chief aims, as we have seen above is to understand how the individual can find the meaning of life in the modern world. Moreover, existentialists hold widely differing views about human existence, and there are a number of recurring themes in their writings.

---

[121] Sartre, *Being and Nothingness*, 620.
[122] Ibid., 707-710.

First, existentialists hold that humans have no predestined purpose or essence laid out for them by God or by nature; it is up to each one of us to decide who and what we are through our own actions. This is the point of Sartre's definition of existentialism; that, for humans, 'existence precedes essence'.[123] What this means is that we first simply exist, and find ourselves born into a world not of our own choosing. And it is then up to each of us to define our own identity or essential characteristics in the course of what we do in living out our lives. Thus, our essence (our set of defining traits) is chosen, not given.

Second, existentialists hold that people decide their own fates and are responsible for what they make of their lives. Humans have free will in the sense that, no matter what social and biological factors influence their decisions, they can reflect on those conditions, decide what they mean, and then make their own choices as to how to handle those factors in acting in the world. Because we are self-creating or self-fashioning beings in this sense, we have full responsibility for what we make of our lives.

Finally, existentialists are concerned with identifying the most authentic and fulfilling way of life possible for individuals. In their view, most of us tend to conform to the ways of living of the 'herd': we feel we are doing well if we do what 'one'

---

[123] Papineau, *Philosophy*, 157.

does in familiar social situations. In this respect, our lives are said to be 'inauthentic,' not really our own. To become authentic, according to this view, an individual must take over his own existence with clarity and intensity. Such a transformation is made possible by such profound emotional experiences as anxiety or the experience of existential guilt (angst). When we face up to what is revealed in such experiences, existentialists claim, we will have a clearer grasp of what is at stake in life, and we will be able to become more committed and integrated individuals.[124]

1.3 Personalistic view

In our day, and all through the history of mankind, there is so much violence in the world, each day we hear about homicides, kidnappings, rapes, abortion, terrorist attacks, hunger, wars and many other forms of threats to human life. It is ironic that, while the human person is the very victim of this violence, it is also the human person who is the agent of such violence. Man is simultaneously becoming the victim and the culprit. As we have seen in the first chapter, man indeed is a paradox, for, while he is bestowed with dignity and good nature, he is also capable of doing evil and inflicting harm against others. This is because he fails to acknowledge the very dignity of his nature as a human person.

---

[124] Papineau, *Philosophy*, 154.

In the first chapter we found the introductory words to the concept of 'human person' and now the attention goes to the thoughts of thinkers who contributed to personalistic approach to find meaning to human life. These thinkers in common share few ideas of existentialistic approach. Their main concern is to defend the inviolable rights and the unique value of man as a human person against the ideologies of Fascism, Nazism and Stalinism in their era, which created a sense of meaninglessness to human life.[125]

Among the prominent thinkers, Emmanuel Mounier, Max Scheller, Martin Buber and Karol Wojtyla stood against all these destructive forms. In their writings the concept 'human person' is reflected in the ideas such as: person as the subject and the object of action, inwardness, openness, situation and the dynamism of personal existence.[126] For instance, Karol Wojtyla recognized the uniqueness of human person as composed of both material and spiritual aspects that makes him unique from all other entities in the world. Moreover he added that, together with the other entities, man can be considered as an object; but because of his nature, the human person is also a subject. As a subject, he is an entity that exists and acts in a certain way, he exists as an object, that is, an objective somebody. Wojtyla clarified:

---

[125] Mercier, *Being Human*, 27-28.
[126] Ibid.

A person is an objective entity, which as a definite subject has the closest contacts with the whole (external) world and is most intimately involved with it precisely because of its inwardness, its interior life. It must be added that it communicates thus not only with the invisible world, and most importantly, with God. This is a further indication of the person's uniqueness in the visible world.[127]

In line with this, Mounier prior to Wojtyla in his treatise, *The Personalism* asserted human embodiment in the following way: "man is a body in the same degree that he is a spirit, wholly body and wholly spirit."[128] Moreover in the first chapter of his book Mounier develops this concept in connection with the inwardness of the human person. He highlights that human person is a self-conscious subjective thinker, who is able to transcend the mere objective existence.[129] Then he clarifies the difference between individualism and personalism. Later he brings into attention the communitarian values of solidarity and inter-relation. In his insistence on inviolable dignity, Mounier resisted

---

[127] Karol Wojtyla, *Love and Responsibility*, tr. in English, H. T. Willets, New York, William Collins Sons and Co. Ltd., 1981, 23.
[128] Emmanuel Mounier, *Personalism*, tr. in English, Philip Mairet, London, Routledge and Kegan Paul Ltd., 1952, 3.
[129] Mounier, *Personalism*, 10 -15.

utilitarianism which would make one person merely "useful" for another. He emphasizes that, whereas individualism places the self above all and views others as means to one's own profit, personalism seeks to make of the self a gift to another. "Thus," Emmanuel Mounier later wrote, "if the first condition of individualism is the centralization of the individual in himself, the first condition of personalism is his decentralization, in order to set him in the open perspectives of personal life."[130] Where individualism hopes to find personal realization in self-interest, personalism asserts the absolute need for openness to others, even as a condition for one's own realization. At the end of his writing he states that one will find meaning to one's life if one lives in communion with the other respecting one's dignity and accepting the other as a human person.[131] This line of thought is quite similar to that of Immanuel Kant who asserted in his concept of practical categorical imperative; "act so as to treat humanity, whether in your own person or in that of another, always as an end and never as a means."[132]

Another prominent thinker who contributed substantially in this approach to finding meaning to life is Martin Buber. He introduced the dialogical concept of the person through his classical explanations of two modes of relationships

---

[130] Mounier, *Personalism*, 20.
[131] Ibid., 114 -120.
[132] Stump, *Philosophy*, 231.

that a human person has with things and other human persons in finding meaning to one's life. According to him, the first mode of relationship characterizes 'I' and 'It'. And in this mode of relationship, the former assumes a possessive monopolizing character. On the other hand, in the 'I-thou' relationship between persons takes a dialogical character with 'encounter, presence, love, freedom and being.'[133] These are the two basic modes of relationships a person can have. At times one could apply the 'I-it' type even in personal relationships where one uses the other as a means to an end.

According to the Buber, it is only in an 'I-thou' relationship that one completes, understands and respects one's own 'I.' Because I have my origin from my relationship with Thou; when I become 'I', then I say 'Thou.'[134] As we have seen above in the beginning of this subheading, all threat to human life and the loss of meaning arise, when human persons are treated as means to an end without proper dignity. Moreover all the personalistic philosophers agree that our unique human nature has the ability to blend one's existential uniqueness with the given 'concrete situatedness'. And they invite us to realize the best meaning to our life that is possible.

---

[133] Martin Buber, *I and Thou*, tr. in English, Ronald Gregor Smith, New York, Charles Scribner's Sons, 1957, 1 - 5.
[134] Ibid., 11.

2. Ultimate meaning is found

As noted above, the persistent 'quest' to know the meaning and purpose of human existence had been a main concern virtually in all the inquiries. Anthropology in particular focuses its full attention on the fundamental quest, in the light of unique human nature we possess in contrast to other kinds of beings and things. Moreover, as we have seen in the first chapter, starting from Socrates' dictum, 'Know Thyself' to the *'Dasein'* of Heidegger, contemporary thinkers have discussed about this quest in some way or the other. Beside the above-mentioned sciences, religions also have substantial answers to the quest for meaning of life.

2.1 Anthropological answer

Anthropology stresses on human quest for never being satisfied with the given facticity. In other words, by our nature, we are restless beings, ever desiring to have more than what we should have. This is one of the reasons for our fundamental quest. This dissatisfaction is manifested basically in three ways. [135]

First, one wants to be more. This desire can be understood as being happier in what one does. Secondly, one desires to know more. This insatiable

---

[135] Mercier, *Being Human*, 73.

quest for knowledge is very evident when we look at the history of human civilization. Finally, one desires values such as justice, peace and love. As anthropologists have noticed, people often misunderstand their quest and embraces the opposite of these values with egoistic attitudes finally falling to individualism. Thus, they tend to acquire more wealth, power and pleasure. [136]

Moreover, with the help of modern thought anthropology recognizes man as a conscious being with freedom and the capacity to transcend any given situation. As stated by Heidegger, the finiteness of human nature places us diverse in situations as we are thrown-in-to-world. In these situations, human beings tend to see the world more disordered and absurd as they live in diverse situations.

One of the best examples is the life of Job in the Bible. Job is portrayed as a just and innocent man, but he is given miseries one after the other for no reason. This makes his life absurd and meaningless.[137] He becomes desperately bewildered and perplexed. At some moments he questions God, and wants to know why he is given such sufferings. As the book further narrates, God speaks to him out of a whirlwind and insists that God's ways are beyond human comprehension. Thus, Job submits himself and accepts the reality as

---

[136] Mercier, *Being Human*, 74.
[137] Job. 6: 9. RSV.

it is. Finally, Job is rewarded for confronting his life's situation.[138]

Another well-known example is the myth of Sisyphus in Greek mythology. The man, Sisyphus is condemned by God to push a rock to the top of a hill, only to see it roll to the bottom time and again. This story is brought to light by the French philosopher, Albert Camus to present the absurdity of human predicament. Camus in his later writings states that despite of this meaninglessness one needs to rebel against the absurdity of life.[139]

Anthropology, with the help of psychology searches the answer to our fundamental quest. Among the eminent psychologists, Viktor Frankl has given a substantial answer to the quest for meaning of human life. He introduced a new theory called logo therapy to find meaning to one's life in drastic situations. He formed this new theory, out of his own experience as a prisoner in a Nazi-death-camp during the Second World War. He illustrates this hellish experience in his celebrated book, *Man's Search for Meaning.* According to Frankl's view, man is neither driven by a will-to-pleasure nor by a will-to-power, but by a will-to-meaning, a deeper striving and a struggle for a higher and ultimate meaning to his existence. Further he states that: "everyone has his own specific vocation or mission

---

[138] Job. 21: 19.
[139] Albert Camus, *The Myth of Sisyphus*, tr. in English, Justin O'Brien, London, Penguin Books, 1955, 107.

in life, and everyone must carry out a concrete assignment that demands fulfilment. Therein he cannot be replaced, nor can his life be repeated. Thus everyone's task is as unique as is specific opportunity to implement it."[140] According to Frankl, as mentioned above, each person has a unique vocation and a mission to fulfil in one's lifespan. For instance, a teacher may find his work in the classroom meaningful, or a parent may describe the project of raising a family as meaningful. Obviously, these projects appear as individual activities, but how can one find the fundamental answer to never ending quest for meaning. It must be more than one's life project or a mission.

2.2 Religious answer

Since the dawn of human existence there had been a quest in human beings to cling on to an ultimate infinite power. It is very clear in *Confessions* of Augustine, when he wrote: "Oh God, thou hast created us for thyself so that our hearts are restless until they find their rest in thee."[141] This quest particularly evolved due to the inevitability of death and the presence of evil in human beings experienced in everyday life.[142] Almost all religions try to interpret death and sufferings according their

---

[140] Frankl, *Man's Search for Meaning in Life*, 172.
[141] Augustine, *The Confessions*, I,1,
[142] Joshtrom Kureethadam, *Creation in Crisis*, New York, Orbis Books, 2014, 45.

beliefs and traditions in order to render meaning to this earthly life.

Religions, moreover, provide a centre of value systems. In defining meaning to one's life, these values give life its fundamental worth. In other words to believe in the supernatural means to have some meaning and value to one's life. According to this perspective, when one loses the belief in the supernatural one quite naturally loses the significance of one's life as well. In modern time many people are despaired not because they do not have values but they have lost the centre of values in their lives; the religious value cord and hope for life after. Moreover, in every religion this value oriented life places a some kind of hope for greater reward and something more than this earthly life, when one end with death.[143] These are the answers given by the world's major religions, in brief.

Hinduism is the world oldest religion, which had begun approximately some five thousand years ago in India.[144] Primarily, it emphasis is not much on its belief, but on human conduct.[145] Moreover it asserts that the aim of one's life is to end the cycle of rebirth and to be reunited with *Brahman* by following one of three paths: work,

---

[143] Singer, *Meaning in Life*, 83.

[144]Martin Baumann, "*Hinduism*" in, Encyclopaedia of Religions of the World, Vol.2, ed., Gordon Melton and Martin Baumann, California, ABC – CLIO Publications, 2002, 586.

[145] Alison Morgan, *What happen When We Die?*, Eastbourne, Kingsway Publications Ltd.,1995. 35.

knowledge or devotion.[146] These three paths have their roots in *Vedas*, *Upanishads* and *Bhakti* respectively. Today most Hindus base their faith on element derived from all the above-mentioned paths. All in all, according to Hinduism, meaning to our earthly life is found through right conduct and selfless works in the hope of attaining salvation from rebirth.[147]

In Buddhism, the starting point is the existence of evil and suffering in the world. It is based on the teaching of Siddhartha Gautama, who lived six centuries before Christ. His aim was to find a remedy for the suffering of the human existence.[148] Therefore the main teaching of Gautama, who became Buddha after enlightenment, is nothing but how to avoid pain, suffering and attain Nirvana. This way he found meaning to earthly existence. Buddhists believe that, there is suffering in the human existence, but one can conquer this, by meditation and following the methods of Buddha, through the "four noble truths."[149] Furthermore according to Buddhism, the cause of all suffering is nothing but the desire in the heart of a human being to have more. Therefore, one must work hard to

---

[146] Alison Morgan, *What happen When We Die?*, Eastbourne, Kingsway Publications Ltd.,1995. 37.

[147] Baumann, "*Hinduism*" in, Encyclopaedia of Religions of the World, Vol. 2, 678.

[148] Morgan, *What happen When We Die?*, 43.

[149] The four noble truths are: 1. Dukkha- Suffering, 2. Samudaya- the arising of dukkha, 3. Nirodha, the cessation of dukkha, 4. Magga- the way leading to the cessation of dukkha.

liberate from this suffering and attain the ultimate goal called Nirvana.[150] Although we have taken Buddhism as a religion for our inquiry, it is noteworthy to mention that, Buddhism is only a moral philosophy. For Buddhists are agnostics, they do not hold any firm belief in god or gods.[151]

Islam, the second largest religion in the world, urges it's faithful to follow five pillars at the heart of their way of life to fulfil the purpose of earthly life. They are as follows: the profession of faith, regular prayer life, pay of special tax, the annual fast in the hours of sunrise and sunset in the month of Ramadan and finally make a visit to Mecca at least once in one's life time. Beside these, some have added the sixth pillar, called *Jihad*. It refers to the obligation of all Muslims to live according to God's will and to promote Islam.[152] The very word Islam means 'Surrender to God's law.' Therefore, for a Muslim the essence of life is to surrender his life to the law of God.[153]

In Christianity, the answer to the meaning of life is based upon the notion of God, whom, the creatures must believe in faith and has devotion to. This is well explained in the words of the *Catechism of the Catholic Church*: "Faith is man's response to

---

[150] Walpola Rahula, *What the Buddha Taught*, Dehiwala, Buddhist Cultural Centre Publication, 1996, 16.

[151] Baumann, "*Buddhism*" in, Encyclopaedia of Religions of the World, Vol. 1, 179.

[152] Morgan, *What Happen When We Die?*, 62-63.

[153] Ibid., 64.

God, who reveals himself and gives himself to man, at the same time bringing man a superabundant light as he searches for the ultimate meaning of his life."[154] In line with this, although humans cannot fully grasp God's ultimate intent for His creation, a life of faith and devotion to Him is considered part of the human purpose for living life. Again, the act of faith alone is not the sole purpose for the Christian life. As mentioned in the scriptures:

> "What good is it, my brothers, if someone says he has faith but does not have works? Can that faith save him? If a brother or sister has nothing to wear and has no food for the day, and one of you says to them, 'Go in peace, keep warm, and eat well,' but you do not give them the necessities of the body, what good is it? So also, faith of itself, if it does not have works, is dead"[155]

Along with faith is also sought the morally virtuous life. This virtuous life, Christ spoke and lived on earth, and encouraged us to do the same. The entire Law of the Gospel is contained in the "New Commandment" of Jesus, to love one another as he has loved us.[156] Christ in his life on earth removed the absurdity of human life when he

---

[154] Catechism of the Catholic Church, 26.
[155] James. 2:14
[156] Jn. 15:12; 13:34.

defeated death by his resurrection giving a new hope and a new life to man.[157]

As we have seen above, all religions have a common ground of offering values to their faithful. But, human tendencies are such, that, how we accept these centres of values. Today with the secularization and due to other circumstances people move away from these centres of values and attempt to quench their never ending 'quest' through deceptive avenues of power, wealth, and pleasure. Christ invited all men to move away from all these deceptive ways of life and to find real meaning in Him, when he said: "I am the way, the truth and life..." [158]

We've added additional text in this section to show you how the headers and footers appear in the subsequent pages. Please delete the instructions and the additional text when you add the actual content of the book.

---

[157] *Phil. 3:8-11.*
[158] *Jn. 14: 6.*

Conclusion

Life's meaning to man becomes absurd, when it is filled with uncertainties, miseries, hatred, sufferings and loss of hope. It becomes all the more meaningless at the face of death, the inevitable. On the contrary, life becomes meaningful, when it is filled with certainties, success, love, happiness and hope. It becomes all the more meaningful in hoping for a life beyond.

In this research, I addressed the problem of "Man's Quest to Know the Meaning of Life," under three chapters. First, in the chapter one, I have presented a brief account on human nature. According to the analysis, man is not just a being reducible to cosmological matter of this world, but a transcendental being, a subject rather an object, who has the capacity to go beyond. Moreover man is more appropriate to be addressed as a 'human person,' because of his rational nature. His rationality is the driving force to question the reality around him and his own life. He asks questions and wants to know what, where, who, how and why of things. As Aristotle stated, by nature we all desire to know, and this quest is inevitable. We cannot neglect this quest. We have to quench this thirst by living the given life.

As our life appears to be a chain of actions, our actions manifest how we respond to the quest. The society where we live recognizes, whether we live meaningful lives through our actions. Accordingly, the meaningful lives and exemplary lives will be remembered and respected forever. For instance, consider the inspiring lives of Francis of Assisi, Don Bosco, Mother Teresa, Mahatma Gandhi, Nelson Mandela, and Pope John Paul II, and many others. On the contrary, think about the people who contributed to the destruction of humanity by abusing their rational power. They used their freewill to opt for genocide, war, violence, abortion and euthanasia, and other forms of destruction.

Furthermore, according to my findings, people behave this way due to lack of proper knowledge about their human nature. With narrow-minded attitude they tend to go behind power, wealth and pleasure, and live meaningless lives. Therefore, to act proper to human nature one must desire to 'know thyself' as Socrates stated.

Every person should make an attempt to know the truth of their lives. Therefore, I began the second chapter, presenting the man's quest for knowledge in the history. Basically, man desires to know the truth of three realities, namely of world, of man and of God. Moreover, in grasping the knowledge about these realities, man realizes that all the sources of knowledge are not reliable. Therefore, he has to looks for reliable sources to arrive at ultimate truth. Here if man takes an extremist approach to attain knowledge and truth, he heads for danger. All the theories cannot be applied for all the above-mentioned realities to understand the truth about them.

In the third chapter, I attempted to answer the fundamental question, "How can Man Find the Meaning in His life?" First, I presented, how modern thinkers viewed human life in their own era. In my analysis, I found that, existentialist thinkers have a common ground in accepting, human beings as free individuals. According to their view, we are free to create meaning of our lives in any given situation, transcending our facticity. Moreover, they refuted that human beings are subjects, and not objects. Agreeing to the subject value of man, all the personalistic thinkers added the absolute need for openness to others, as a condition for one's own realization. They further asserted that, meaning to life is found, when one lives in communion with the other respecting one's dignity and accepting the other as a human person.

Second, I focussed on the anthropological and religious answers to the ultimate question. Anthropology points out how we tend to fall into existential vacuum, without accepting life's struggles and sufferings. Moreover, anthropology with the help of psychological findings indicates how important our will-to-meaning is. We tend to give up this will-to-meaning when we lose hope. Hope lasts as long as we have something to live for. This something can be our specific vocation, family, values, or it can be a hope for a life beyond. People who lose hope and neglect the quest step into the abyss of destructive behaviour.

Finally, I considered the answers given by four major religions. All the major religions, I have discussed, have an answer to the fundamental question. Hinduism and Buddhism in common find the meaning of life through the cessation of rebirth. According to their view, to end the circle of rebirth one must live a virtuous life.

In Christianity and Islam, meaning of life is found in knowing and worshiping the true God. To know Him and to worship Him, one must have faith in Him. Having faith in Him means to surrender oneself. In Islam, surrendering oneself to God is equivalent to surrendering to the law of God. Therefore, according to Islam, only righteous people find the meaning of life. According to Christianity, faith is man's response to God. Christian faith calls people to live virtuous and righteous lives as Christ lived and to hope for life eternal.

All in all, having discussed the problem of "Man's Quest to Know the Meaning" from a different perspective, I realize, the reason for his insatiable quest. As we have seen above, it is his unique human nature, and the rationality that question the reality and the purpose of his own existence. To live proper to our human nature we must quench this quest. Therefore, we have to continue our quest for knowledge and truth until we arrive at it. We must try to attain the true knowledge, because the object of our knowledge becomes a part of our life. The more we desire know the reality, the more we discover our uniqueness and the meaning.

Finally, I would suggest that, the meaning of life is found, when one bases one's life in the centre of values. The centre of values can be found in a true religion. Christianity, for instance, helps one to live an authentic life, accepting one's capacities and limitations. Respecting and promoting the dignity of one's own life and that of the other. It guides our lives with the code of love. It transforms our life's sufferings and miseries into meaningful sacrifices. Ultimately, it helps us to quench the quest by defeating the inevitable death, which denies the meaning of life, and ushering for a new life that make our life meaningful.

BIBLIOGRAPHY

A. Primary Sources

Aquinas, Thomas, *Summa Theologiae,* Latin-English Edition of the Works of St. Thomas Aquinas, tr. Laurence Shapcote, ed. John Mortensen and Enrique Alarcon, Vol. 13-20, *Corpus Thomisticun Opera Omnia*, Leoniene Edtition, Lander, Wyoming, The Aquinas Institute of the Study of Sacred Doctrine, 2012.

Arendt, Hannah, *The Human Condition*, 2nd ed., with an introduction by Margaret Canova, London, The University of Chicago Press Ltd., 1998.

Aristotle, *De Anima*, tr. in English, Hugh Lawson, London, Penguin Books ltd., 1986.

---, *The Metaphysics*, tr. in English and ed., Hugh Lawson, London, Penguin Books Ltd., 2004.

----, *The Nicomachean Ethics*, Aristotle's Ethics, tr. in English J.A. K. Thomson, London, Penguin Books Ltd., 1955.

Augustine, *The Confessions* tr. in English, Tobie Matthew, ed., Roder Huddleston, London, Fontana Books, 1963.

Bali, Raj, *Introduction to Philosophy,* 2 ed., New Delhi, Sterling Publishers, 1997.

Bescherevnykh, E., *The Secret of Man's Being*, Moscow, Novartis Press Agency House, 1972.

Boss, Judith A., *Ethics for Life,* London, Mayfield Publication Company, 1998.

Buber, Martin, *I and Thou*, tr. in English, Ronald Gregor Smith, New York, Charles Scribner's Sons, 1957.

Camus, Albert, The Myth of Sisyphus, tr. in English, Justin O'Brien, London, Penguin Books, 1955.

Catechism of the Catholic Church, New Delhi, Theological Publications India, 1994.

Copleston, Frederick, *A History of Philosophy,* Vol. 1, *Greece and Rome; From the Pre-Socratic to Plotinus,* New York, Bantam Doubleday publishers, 1993.

---, *A History of Philosophy,* Vol. 3, *Late Medieval and Renaissance Philosophy,* New York, Bantam Doubleday Publishers, 1993.

---, *A History of Philosophy*, vol. 5, *Modern philosophy: The British Philosophers from Hobbes to Hume*, New York, Bantam Doubleday publishers, 1993.

Descartes, *Meditations on the First Philosophy*, tr. in English and revised by Deena Weinberg, New York, BN Publishers, 2007.

Folliet, Joseph, *Man in Society*, London, William Clowes Limited, 1963.

Frankl, Viktor, *Man's Search for Meaning in Life*, tr. in English, Ilse Lasch, New York, Washington Square Press, 1959.

Fromm, Erich, *To Have or to Be?,* ed., Ruth Nanda, New York, Harper and Row Publication, 1976.

Gilson, Etienne, *Methodical Realism, A Hand Book for Beginning Realists*, tr. in English, Philip Trower, San Francisco, Ignatius Press Publication, 2011.

Heidegger, Martin, *Being and Time*, tr. in English, John Macquarie and Robinson, Oxford, Basil Blackwell Publishers Ltd., 1962.

Higgins, Thomas J., *Man as Man; the Science and Art of Ethics*, Rockford, Tan Books and Publishers, 1992.

John Paul II, *Veritatis Splendor*, The Modern World and Contemporary Moral Theology, Vatican City, Liberia Editrice Vaticana, 1996.

Kandakavil, Thomas, *Ethical World, A Study on the Ethical Thought in the West and the East*, Banglore, Darmaram Publications, 1995.

Kreeft, Peter, *Human Person; Catholic Christianity*, The Luke E. Heart Series, New York, Catholic Information Publication, 2001.

Kureethadam, Joshtrom, *Creation in Crisis*, New York, Orbis Books, 2014.

Kvanvig, Jonathan L., *The Value of Knowledge and the Pursuit of Understanding,* New York, Cambridge University Press, 2003.

Leister, Brian, *The Future for Philosophy*, New York, Oxford University Publication, 2006.

Leslie, Stevenson and Haberman D.L., *Ten Theories of Human Nature*, New York, Oxford University Press, 1998.

Locke, John, *An Essay Concerning Human Understanding,* ed. and intro. by John w. Yolton, London, J.M. Dent Ltd, 1992.

Macquarie, John, *Existentialism*, New York, The World Publishing Company, 1979.

Marcel, Gabriel, *Being and Having,* London, Collins Clear- Type Press Publication, 1965.

Mercier, Jean L., *Being Human,* Bangalore: Asian Trading Cooperation, 1998.

Mirandola, Pico Della, *On the Dignity of Man,* tr. in English, Charles Glenn and Douglas Carmichael, Cambridge, Hackett Publishing Company, 1998.

Morgan, Alison, *What happen When We Die?, Eastbourne, Kingsway Publications Ltd.,* 1995.

Mounier, Emmanuel, *Personalism*, tr. in English, Philip Mairet, London, Routledge and Kegan Paul Ltd., 1952.

Olsen, Allene, *Evolution, Creationism, and Intelligent Design*, California, Green Wood Publishers, 2010.

Olson, Steve, *Mapping Human History*, London, Bloomsbury Publishing, 2002.

Papineau, David, *Philosophy: The Illustrated Guide to Understanding and Using Philosophy Today,* London: Duncan Baird Publishes, 2004.

Radhakrishnan and Raju, P., *The Concept Of Man: The Concept of Man in Greek Thought,* New Delhi, Harper Collins Publishers India, 1997.

Rahula, Walpola, *What the Buddha Taught,* Dehiwala, Buddhist Cultural Centre Publication, 1996.

Reinhardt, Kurt F., *The Existentialist Revolt, The Main Themes and Phases of Existentialism*, California, The Bruce Publishing Company, 1952.

Rescher, Nicholas, *Epistemology, An Introduction to the Theory of Knowledge,* New York, A State University of New York Press, 2003.

Russell, Bertrand, *A History Western Philosophy*, London, George Allen and Unwin Brothers Ltd, 1947.

---, *The Problems of Philosophy*, New Delhi, Oxford University Press, 2003.

Sartre, Jean P., *Being and Nothingness*, tr. in English, Hazel E. Barnes, New York, Washington Square Publication, 1956.

Savundar, Edwin, *The Philosophy of form and Human Person*, New York, Wisdom Publications, 2004.

Schick, Moritz, *General Theory of Knowledge*, tr. in English, E. Blumberg, New York, Herbert Hansberger Publication, 1974.

Schroeder, William R., *Continental Philosophy, a Critical Approach*, Oxford, Blackwell Publishers, 2005.

Second Vatican council, *Gaudium et Spes*, the Pastoral Constitution of the Church in the Modern World, ed. Austin Flannery, *Vatican Council II*, Bombay, St. Paul Publications, 1975.

Singer, Irving, *Meaning in Life: The Harmony of Nature and Spirit*, Vol. 1, London, The Mit press, 2010.

Stumpf, Samuel E., *Philosophy: History and Problems,* 5th ed., New York, McGraw- hill Publications, 1994.

Sullivan, Daniel J., *An Introduction to Philosophy*, New York, The Bruce Publishing Company, 1957.

Titus, Harold H., *Ethics for Today*, 3rd ed., New Delhi, Eurasia Publishing House Private Limited, 1996.

Wojtyla, Karol, *Love and Responsibility*, tr. in English, H. T. Willets, New York, William Collins Sons and Co. Ltd., 1981.

Young, Christen C. and Largent, Mark A., *Evolution and Creationism*, London: Green Wood Press, 2007.

B. SECONDARY SOURCES

Arthur, Paul, and Lewis Edwin, *The Library of Living Philosophers*, Vol. 17, *The Philosophy of Gabriel Marcel,* Illinois, Open Court Publishing Company, 1991.

Dicker, Georges, *Kant's Theory of Knowledge: An Analytical Introduction,* New York, Oxford University Press, 2004.

Francisco, Roland B., *Karol Wojtyla's Theory of Participation: Based on His Christian Personalism,* Manila, St. Paul's Publications, 1995.

Hamlyn, D.W., "Aristotle on Dialectics", *Aristotle: A Biography of His Visions and Ideas*, ed. Subrata Mukherjee and Sushila Ramaswamy, New Delhi, Deep and Deep Publications, 1998.

Kanti, Mrinal, *Critical Survey of Phenomenology and Existentialism,* New Delhi, Allied Publishers Limited, 1990.

Kaufman, Walter, *Existentialism from Dostoevsky to Sartre*, New York, The World Publishing Company, 1969.

Kemp, Norman, *A Commentary to Kant's Critique of Pure Reason*, New York, Palgrave Macmillan Ltd., 2003.

Sparshott, F. E., "Plato as a Political Thinker", *Plato: A Biography of His Visions and Ideas*, ed. Subrata Mukherjee and Sushila Ramaswamy, New Delhi, Deep and Deep Publications, 1998.

Stevens, Anthony, *On Jung,* London, Rutledge Publishers, 1990.

C. ARTICLES

Angus, Robert, "Industrial Revolution and Its Impact" in, *Encyclopedia Britannica,* Vol. 28, 15th ed. Chicago, Encyclopaedia Britannica publishers, 1997, 453- 472.

Baumann, Martin "Hinduism" in, *Encyclopaedia of Religions of the World,* Vol.2, ed., Gordon Melton and Martin Baumann, California, ABC – CLIO Publications, 2002, 586- 596.

Baumann, Martin, "Buddhism" in, *Encyclopaedia of Religions of the World,* Vol.1, ed., Gordon Melton and Martin Baumann, California, ABC – CLIO Publications, 2002, 179-198.

Bruce, Russell, "Intuition" in, *The Cambridge Dictionary of Philosophy*, New York, Cambridge University press, 1995, 382.

Graff, Hilda, "Mystical Knowledge" in, *The Catholic Encyclopaedia for Schools and Homes*, Thomas E. Dubay, New York, McGraw-Hill Publishers, 1965, 7: 411-412.

Holmes, Robert L.,"Gandhi, Mohandas Karaenchand," *The Cambridge Dictionary of Philosophy*, gen. ed. Robert Audi, New York, Cambridge University Press, 1995, 293.

Paul, George, "Philosophical Anthropology" in, *Encyclopedia Britannica,* Vol. 25,15th ed. Chicago, Encyclopaedia Britannica publishers, 1997, 550-561.

Safra, Jacob. E, "The Genocide" in, *Encyclopaedia Britannica,* in, *Encyclopedia Britannica,* Vol. 5,15th ed. Chicago, Encyclopaedia Britannica publishers, 1997, 183.

Stroll, Avrum, "Epistemology" in, *Encyclopaedia Britannica*, Vol. 18, 15th ed. Chicago, Encyclopaedia Britannica publishers, 1997, 466-488.

Urry, James, "History of Anthropology" in, *The Routledge Encyclopaedia of Social and Cultural Anthropology,* 2nd ed. Alan Barnard and Jonathan Spencer, New York, Routledge Publishers, 2010, 348-351.

Souza, Savio D', "The Personalist Christian View of Emmanuel Mounier," *Divyadaan*, Vol. 25, 2, 2014, 181-202.